ENTERTAINMENT'S

TOP 10

MUSIC AND THEATER TOP TENS

SANDY DONOVAN

Lerner Publications Company • Minneapolis

NOTE TO READERS: You'll find a lot of popular songs mentioned in this book. But before you start downloading, remember to check advisory guidelines and buy music only with a parent's or guardian's permission.

All of the lists in this book, as well as the data used to compile them, are current as of the time this publication went to press.

Lerner Publications Company
A division of Lerner Publishing Group, Inc.
241 First Avenue North
Minneapolis, MN 55401 USA

For reading levels and more information, look up this title at www.lernerbooks.com.

Library of Congress Cataloging-in-Publication Data

Donovan, Sandra, 1967–
     Music and theater top tens / by Sandy Donovan.
       pages   cm. — (Entertainment's top 10)
     Includes index.
     ISBN 978–1–4677–3843–9 (lib. bdg. : alk. paper)
     ISBN 978–1–4677–4675–5 (eBook)
     1. Popular music—Juvenile literature. 2. Musicians—Juvenile literature.
     3. Theater—New York (State)—New York—Juvenile literature. I. Title.
     ML3470.D66 2015
     781.640973—dc23   2013046317

Manufactured in the United States of America
1 – VI – 7/15/14

TABLE OF CONTENTS

INTRODUCTION

Are you a fan of music? Theater? How about musical theater? If the answer to any of these questions is yes, then this is the book for you! It's full of lists of the very best from the world of music and the stage.

Each list is put together using facts and stats, so you know it's the real deal. You'll find out which performers sold the most digital singles and which Broadway shows have stood the test of time. You'll find lists of award-winning musicians, actors, and directors. Turn the page to start counting down some of music and theater's top performers, shows, and more!

Katy Perry sells out arenas on tour, but how do her digital music sales rank among musicians? Read on to find out!

MUSICIANS WITH THE MOST DIGITAL SINGLES SALES

Once upon a time, musicians sold their music mostly on albums—on CD, cassette, eight-track tape or, if you go way back, vinyl. Musicians still put albums together, but they count on selling digital singles to get their sound in the ears of the most fans. Below, we count down the artists who've sold the most digital singles, according to stats from the Recording Industry Association of America (RIAA).

10. Carrie Underwood: >>>> 22.5 million sales

After shooting to fame as the winner of *American Idol* in 2005, this country music star from Oklahoma proved her sticking power with fans. With six Grammy Awards, 16 Billboard Music Awards, and 10 Academy of Country Music Awards to her name, she's often called country music's reigning queen. Her hits include "Before He Cheats," "Cowboy Casanova," and "Blown Away."

9. Lil Wayne: 23.5 million sales

This hip-hop artist from New Orleans (born Dwayne Michael Carter Jr.) has been in the spotlight since releasing his first solo album in 1999. He's gotten his largest digital sales for "Down," "Lollipop," and "Let It Rock."

8. Justin Bieber: 24 million sales

Discovered at the age of 13 when a talent agent stumbled across his YouTube video, this Canadian singer quickly became a teen sensation. With millions of fans who dub themselves Beliebers, he's mobbed everywhere he goes. His biggest-selling singles? "Boyfriend," "Baby," and "Never Say Never."

7. and 6. (tie!)
Kanye West: 27 million sales

With seven studio albums between 2004 and 2013, this hip-hop legend had a total of six singles break 500,000 sales. No. 1 singles "Stronger" and "Gold Digger" brought him his biggest digital sales.

Bruno Mars: 27 million sales

Hawaiian singer-songwriter Mars got his digital sales off to a good start with his 2010 debut album *Doo-Wops & Hooligans*, which featured three hit singles: "Just the Way You Are," "Grenade," and "The Lazy Song." His second album, 2012's *Unorthodox Jukebox*, included two more huge-selling singles, "Locked Out of Heaven" and "When I Was Your Man."

Bruno Mars (center) performs during the Super Bowl Halftime Show on February 2, 2014.

5. Flo Rida: >>>>>> 27.5 million sales

Born Tramar Dillard, this singer-songwriter took his stage name from his native state when he hit the hip-hop scene in 2006. His collaborations with T-Pain (on "Low") and Ke$ha (on "Right Round") both broke digital sales records for the weeks they were released. Other big sellers include "Club Can't Handle Me," "Good Feeling," and "Wild Ones."

4. Lady Gaga: 28.5 million sales

Gaga (real name: Stefani Germanotta) first snagged the spotlight with her 2008 debut album *The Fame*. Two international No. 1 hits on that album—"Just Dance" and "Poker Face"—set her on the road to digital sales records. She boosted her spot on this list with sales of her later smash hits, including "Bad Romance," "Telephone," "Born This Way," and "Do What U Want."

3. Katy Perry: 29.5 million sales

Since her big break in 2008, the California-based singer-songwriter logged chart-topping sales for a long string of hits. From "Hot n Cold" (2008) and "Firework" (2010) to "Dark Horse" (2013) and "Roar" (2013), her digital singles have stayed at the front of the pack.

2. Rihanna: 44.5 million sales

From her seven studio albums, Rihanna has seen 13 singles reach the top of the *Billboard* Hot 100 chart. The singer, actress, and fashion icon has sold more than 44 million digital singles since releasing her first album in 2005. Megahits include "SOS," "Umbrella," "Don't Stop the Music," "Rude Boy," and "Stay."

1. Taylor Swift: 45 million sales

Swift was just 17 when she released the self-titled debut album that launched her career. Since then she's won seven Grammy Awards, 15 American Music Awards, and 12 Billboard Music Awards. She claimed first place on this list with sales from hits such as "We Are Never Ever Getting Back Together," "Mine," "I Knew You Were Trouble," and "Red."

Taylor performs her hit song "Red" during the CMA Music Festival in June 2013.

Ah, Broadway! This little stretch of Manhattan's Theater District can host up to 40 different musicals a night. Once a show opens, it's up to fans to determine how long its run will be. Some disastrous shows close after the first night. Others play to packed theaters for years. Here, we count down the most popular Broadway shows, based on how long they held audiences captive.

10. *Mamma Mia!*: 12+ years

Since October 2001, this musical based on songs by the super group ABBA has charmed Broadway theatergoers. The show includes hit tunes such as "Dancing Queen," "Take a Chance on Me," and "Thank You for the Music." It also inspired the 2008 film version starring Amanda Seyfried.

9. *Rent*: 12 years, 5 months

This rock musical, inspired by the opera *La Bohème*, tells the story of a group of starving young artists in 1980s New York City. It wowed audiences from April 1996 to September 2008. During that time, it won a Grammy Award for Best Musical Show Album, the Pulitzer Prize for Drama, and four Tony Awards.

Cast members of *Rent* perform the song "La Vie Bohème" in 2008.

8. *Oh! Calcutta!*: 12 years, 10 months

After flopping in its first Broadway stint (1971–1972), this boundary-pushing show was revived for another run in September 1976. This time, it took New York City by storm. It's the longest-running revue—a type of musical theater that includes small skits along with music and dance—in Broadway history.

7. *Beauty and the Beast*: 13 years, 3 months

Based loosely on a French fairy tale but specifically on Disney's 1991 animated movie, *Beauty and the Beast* tells the story of a prince-turned-beast who must win the love of a beautiful young woman. In addition to its long Broadway run—April 1994 to July 2007—*Beauty* has played in more than 100 cities around the world.

6. *A Chorus Line*: 14 years, 9 months

A Broadway show about Broadway is as meta as it gets. This musical features a group of dancers auditioning for spots on a chorus line (a team of synchronized dancers). It filled seats from July 1975 to April 1990—and came back for a Broadway revival in 2006. In 1976 the show snagged nine Tony awards, including best musical, as well as the Pulitzer Prize for Drama.

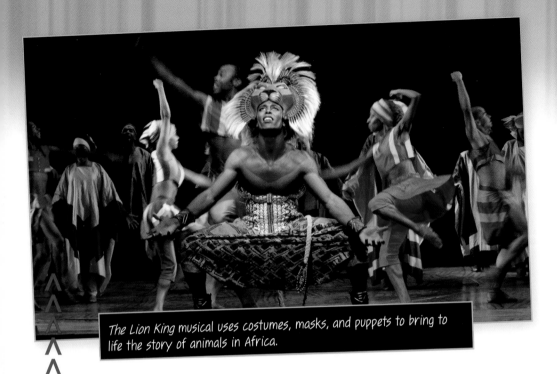

The Lion King musical uses costumes, masks, and puppets to bring to life the story of animals in Africa.

5. *The Lion King*: 16+ years

This show has been a Broadway king since it opened in November 1997. Based on the 1994 animated Disney movie of the same name, the show features music by Elton John. It won six Tony Awards in 1998, including Best Musical, plus the 1999 Grammy Award for Best Musical Show Album. In 2012 it also became the highest-grossing Broadway show of all time, with total earnings of more than $853 million.

4. *Les Misérables*: 16 years, 2 months

Audiences savored every minute of the three-hour-long *Les Mis* from March 1987 to May 2003. Its epic story, based on Victor Hugo's classic novel, follows French peasant and ex-criminal Jean Valjean as he gets swept up in a revolution. The show won nine Tony Awards in 1987, including Best Musical. It also landed the 1988 Grammy Award for Best Musical Cast Show Album.

3. *Chicago*: 17+ years

Set in the title city in the 1920s, this musical showcases the dreams and schemes of criminals, jailers, and lawyers. Based on a play of the same name written by a Chicago crime reporter in 1926, it continues to excite fans. The original Broadway production ran from 1975 to 1977. The still-successful revival premiered in November 1996.

This saga of a fictional tribe of cats is based on *Old Possum's Book of Practical Cats* by T. S. Eliot. The show features the hit song "Memory" and other classics by composer Andrew Lloyd Webber. Though its nearly 18-year run on Broadway (October 1982 to September 2000) is nothing to sneeze at, its run in London was even longer—21 years (1981–2002)!

1. *Phantom of the Opera*: 26+ years

Since January 1988, the Majestic Theatre has been home to this musical based on a 1910 French novel. The show tells the story of a beautiful opera singer and the twisted musical genius who is obsessed with her. The show netted seven Tony Awards in 1988, including Best Musical.

YOUNGEST MUSICIANS TO WIN A GRAMMY AWARD

There are lots of ways to rank musicians: songs recorded, records sold, awards won. When it comes to music awards, the Grammy Awards are the cream of the crop. To score even one Grammy over the course of a long career is a huge accomplishment. But some artists have landed Grammy Awards at the very beginning of their careers—when they're still young adults or even teenagers. Below, we count down the youngest artists to ever receive this award.

10. Brandy: 20 years, 13 days

Brandy Norwood launched her musical and acting career in 1994 at the age of 15. In 1999 she won her first Grammy just after turning 20. She took home Best R&B Performance by a Duo or Group with Vocals for her duet with Monica, "The Boy Is Mine." By then Brandy was already a household name thanks to her role as the title character in the sitcom *Moesha*. She continues to sing and act. Her sixth album, *Two Eleven*, was an R&B hit in 2012.

9. Rihanna: 19 years, 356 days

By the time she won her first Grammy in 2008, the teen sensation from Barbados had already made her mark with hits such as "SOS" and "Unfaithful." That year she was nominated for four Grammys and won Best Rap/Song Collaboration for her hit single "Umbrella," sung with superstar Jay-Z. She's gone on to win five more Grammy Awards and land 12 No. 1 singles on the *Billboard* Hot 100 chart.

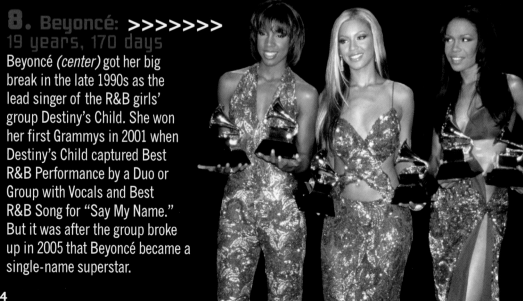

8. Beyoncé: >>>>>>>> 19 years, 170 days

Beyoncé *(center)* got her big break in the late 1990s as the lead singer of the R&B girls' group Destiny's Child. She won her first Grammys in 2001 when Destiny's Child captured Best R&B Performance by a Duo or Group with Vocals and Best R&B Song for "Say My Name." But it was after the group broke up in 2005 that Beyoncé became a single-name superstar.

7. Joss Stone: 19 years, 156 days

This British soul singer, songwriter, and actress hit the music scene in late 2003 with her multi-platinum debut album, *The Soul Sessions*. Four years later, she won Best R&B Performance by a Duo or Group with Vocals for "Family Affair" with John Legend and Van Hunt. In all, she's released six albums in between acting gigs.

6. Alison Krauss: 19 years, 150 days

This bluegrass singer, songwriter, and fiddle player got an early start as a performer. She won a talent contest at the age of 10 and began recording music when she was 14. In 1991 she took home her first Grammy for *I've Got That Old Feeling*. She's won 27 Grammy Awards and is tied (with Quincy Jones) for the second most Grammy Awards ever won by a nonclassical artist. She's also released 14 albums, which have helped popularize bluegrass music in the United States.

<<< 5. Christina Aguilera: 19 years, 67 days

Aguilera first took to the stage at the age of 13 as part of *The All New Mickey Mouse Club*. The popular kids' show teamed her with budding stars Justin Timberlake, Britney Spears, and Ryan Gosling. In 1999, at 18, she released her self-titled debut album, which came in at No. 1 on the *Billboard* chart. The next year, she won the Grammy Award for Best New Artist. She's followed up her early success with six best-selling albums.

4. Monica: 18 years, 123 days

Monica Denise Brown was traveling in a gospel choir by the age of 10. In 1995, at 14, she released her debut album, *Miss Thang*. Four years later, she won Best R&B Performance by a Duo or Group with Vocals for "The Boy Is Mine," her duet with Brandy. That song, plus her album of the same name, made Monica an international star. After an unsuccessful follow-up album in 2002, Monica released four more albums that all cracked the top 10 on the *Billboard* charts.

3. Lorde: >>>>>> 17 years, 80 days

New Zealander Ella Yelich-O'Connor *(right)* was an avid reader and poet before she started writing songs at the ripe old age of 13. By the time she was 16, Ella had become Lorde. With a mix of indie pop and electronica, plus a dash of soul, Lorde's debut album, *Pure Heroine* (2013), was an instant chart topper. In 2014 Lorde nabbed four Grammys— Best Pop Vocal Album along with Record of the Year, Best Pop Solo Performance, and Song of the Year for her hit single "Royals."

2. Luis Miguel: 14 years, 313 days

This Mexican singer and superstar is often called El Sol de México (the Su
Mexico). Miguel first performed professionally at 11 years old. In 1984 he
his first Grammy at 14 for his duet "Me Gustas Tal Como Eres" (I Like You
the Way You Are) with Sheena Easton. He reached international superstard
in the 1990s and is one of the most widely touring and best-selling Latin
artists of all time.

1. LeAnn Rimes:
14 years, 182 days

Child country star LeAnn Rimes was only 14 when she won her first
two Grammys in 1997: Best New Artist and Best Female Country Voca
Performance for "Blue." She also became the first country artist to w
the Best New Artist Grammy. She crossed over from country to pop m
in the late 1990s and has kept branching out ever since. She's release
albums, starred in TV series and films, and written four books.

What makes a Broadway performance really shine? Is it the songs? The stars? The writing? In fact, all these elements are critical to a show's success. And the theater's highest awards honor contributions from each area. Here we count down the 10 top winners of Tony Awards—or, if you want to be formal, the Antoinette Perry Awards for Excellence in Theatre. Check out the people who've won the most awards (not counting Special Tony Awards for Lifetime Achievement). For ties, we've listed the winners alphabetically.

10., **9.**, **8.**, and **7.** (four-way tie!)
Tom Stoppard: 5 awards

Playwright Tom Stoppard has written some of Broadway's most loved plays. And although there's no Tony Award for Authors, Best Play awards are presented to both the play's author and the director, so those are the awards counted here. Stoppard has won that award four times—for *Rosencrantz and Guildenstern Are Dead* (1968), *Travesties* (1976), *The Real Thing* (1984), and the three-part *The Coast of Utopia* (2007). *The Real Thing* also earned him an award for Best Revival of a Play when it was brought back to Broadway in 2000.

Audra McDonald won a Tony Award for her performance in *Porgy and Bess*, an opera about love and loss.

Audra McDonald: 5 awards

McDonald first appeared on Broadway in 1992, and within six years, she had won three Tony Awards—for her roles in *Carousel*, *Master Class*, and *Ragtime*. Since then she's taken home two more Tonys: one for *A Raisin in the Sun* (2004) and one for *Porgy and Bess* (2012). She's also an accomplished singer, with several albums and opera performances on her résumé. Offstage, she starred in the medical drama TV series *Private Practice* from 2007 to 2011.

Angela Lansbury: 5 awards

British actress Angela Lansbury has logged more than seven decades as a star of stage, film, and TV. Her five Tony Awards were for performances in *Mame* (1966), *Dear World* (1969), *Gypsy* (1975), *Sweeney Todd* (1979), and *Blithe Spirit* (2009). In film, Lansbury won three Academy Awards for Best Supporting Actress, and on TV she starred in the murder-mystery series *Murder, She Wrote* from 1984 to 1996.

Julie Harris: 5 awards

Actress Julie Harris holds the record for most Tony Award nominations of any actress (10). She won half of them, for *I Am a Camera* (1952), *The Lark* (1956), *Forty Carats* (1969), *The Last of Mrs. Lincoln* (1973), and *The Belle of Amherst* (1977). Harris also acted in movies, including 1955's *East of Eden*, and on TV, notably in the 1980s series *Knott's Landing*. In 2002 she received a Special Tony Award for Lifetime Achievement.

6. Stephen Sondheim: 7 awards

Though the legendary composer and lyric writer wrote music and lyrics for dozens of shows from the 1950s onward, he's best known for his work in the 1970s with director Hal Prince. In 1971 Sondheim scored his first two Tonys, Best Music and Best Lyrics, for *Company*. (That was the only year the Best Original Score award was split into two categories.) Since then he's won Best Original Score for *Follies* (1972), *A Little Night Music* (1973), *Sweeney Todd* (1979), *Into the Woods* (1988), and *Passion* (1994).

Stephen Sondheim (right) had such success on Broadway with Sweeney Todd that it was made into a 2007 film starring Johnny Depp and Helena Bonham Carter (sitting to Sondheim's left).

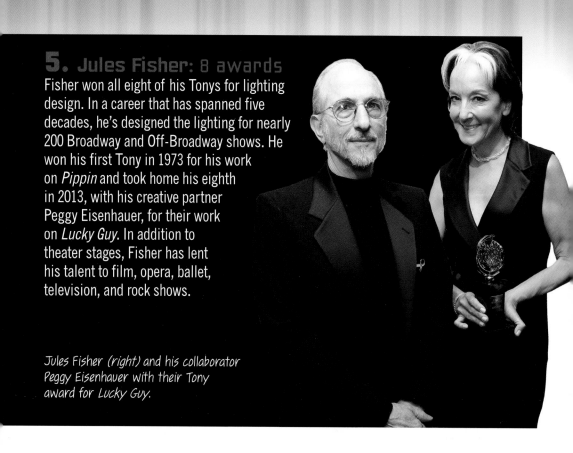

5. Jules Fisher: 8 awards

Fisher won all eight of his Tonys for lighting design. In a career that has spanned five decades, he's designed the lighting for nearly 200 Broadway and Off-Broadway shows. He won his first Tony in 1973 for his work on *Pippin* and took home his eighth in 2013, with his creative partner Peggy Eisenhauer, for their work on *Lucky Guy*. In addition to theater stages, Fisher has lent his talent to film, opera, ballet, television, and rock shows.

Jules Fisher (right) and his collaborator Peggy Eisenhauer with their Tony award for Lucky Guy.

4., 3., and 2. (three-way tie!)
Tommy Tune: 9 awards

When it comes to Broadway shows, Tune has done it all. He's an actor, singer, dancer, director, producer, and choreographer. He won his first Tony Award for Best Featured Actor in a Musical for his role in *Seesaw*. In all, his Tony haul includes four awards for choreography, three for directing, and two for performing.

Oliver Smith: 9 awards

As a Broadway scenic designer from the 1940s to the early 1990s, Smith worked on dozens of famous productions. He earned his first Tony Award for his design work on the set of 1957's *My Fair Lady*. The rest of his awards were also for scenic design on shows including *West Side Story* (1958), *The Sound of Music* (1960), and *Hello, Dolly!* (1964).

Bob Fosse: 9 awards

Perhaps Broadway's most famous choreographer, Fosse is known for his unique jazz dance style. His career also included acting, dancing, and directing both theater and movies. Eight of Fosse's Tony Awards were for choreography, and one was earned for directing. He also won an Academy Award for directing the 1973 film *Cabaret*.

Bob Fosse (front center) rehearses jazz hands with fellow dancers. Fosse's choreography often included jazz hands, rolled shoulders, and hip thrusts.

1. Harold Prince: 18 awards

Hal Prince began working as a theatrical producer on Broadway in the 1950s. In the decades since then, he's directed or produced dozens of acclaimed musicals, including *Cabaret, Sweeney Todd, Evita,* and *Kiss of the Spider Woman*. In addition to 10 Tony Awards for producing and eight for directing, he's won three Special Tony Awards for Lifetime Achievement.

MUSICIANS WITH THE MOST MTV VIDEO MUSIC AWARDS

Music is awesome, right? And video? Pretty awesome too. It's no surprise that when you combine the two, magic can happen. But how do you tell the best from the rest? Each year, MTV tries to do just that as it honors standout music videos. Below, we count down the bands who've won the most MTV Video Music Awards since the channel started handing them out in 1984.

10. and 9. (tie)
TLC: 5 awards
<<< This hip-hop trio *(left)* released 20 videos between 1992 and 2003. In that time, the group also had 10 top 10 singles, four No. 1 singles, and five Grammy Awards. They earned four 1995 MTV awards for "Waterfalls," including Video of the Year. Four years later, they won Best Group Video for "No Scrubs."

No Doubt: 5 awards
This Southern California band featuring Gwen Stefani on vocals has been labeled everything from punk to new wave to pop to classic rock. Whatever their style, their videos have been a hit with fans since their first effort, 1992's "Trapped in a Box." They won their five MTV awards for 1997's "Don't Speak," 2002's "Hey Baby," and 2004's "It's My Life."

8. U2: 6 awards

Together since 1976, this Irish rock group has released 12 albums and more than 60 music videos. They won their first MTV award, Viewer's Choice, for 1987's "With or Without You." In 2001 they received the channel's Video Vanguard Award, also known as the Lifetime Achievement Award, for their career impact on MTV culture.

7., 6., and 5. (three-way tie)
Smashing Pumpkins: 7 awards

This alternative rock band from Chicago formed in 1988 but hit it big with their third album in 1995, *Mellon Collie and the Infinite Sadness*. They won all seven of their MTV awards for songs from that album, including Video of the Year for "Tonight, Tonight."

Red Hot Chili Peppers: 7 awards

Five high school friends from Los Angeles launched this rock/funk band in 1983. They released four albums and built a strong cult following before their fifth record topped the charts in 1991. Videos from their hits "Under the Bridge" and "Give It Away" earned the band their first two MTV awards. They won three more in 2000 and another in 2006.

*NSync: 7 awards

This boy band featuring Justin Timberlake topped the pop charts in the late 1990s and the early 2000s. Three of their Video Music Awards were for 2000's "Bye Bye Bye," and the other four honored 2001's "Pop." Although they released their last album in 2001, the members regrouped in August 2013 to perform at that year's MTV Video Music Awards.

4. A-ha: 8 awards

This pop band from Norway hit it big with their debut album in 1985. The album's two hit songs—"Take On Me" and "The Sun Always Shines on TV"—helped the band capture six MTV awards at the 1986 ceremony. The album also earned them a Grammy Award nomination as Best New Artist. Though the band played together into the 2000s and released eight more albums, they never matched that early success.

3. Aerosmith: 10 awards

Lead vocalist Steven Tyler and his blues-based American hard rock band have been topping the charts since the 1970s. They won their first two video awards in 1990 for their "Janie's Got a Gun" video. They went on to bring home trophies in 1991, 1993, 1994, 1997, and 1998.

2. Green Day: 11 awards

This California punk rock band has been making records since 1987. They were underground favorites for years until they scored big with their first major label record in 1994. Four years later, they took home their first MTV Video Award, Best Alternative Video for "Time of Your Life (Good Riddance)." They came back to win seven awards for 2005's "Boulevard of Broken Dreams" and another three for 2009's "21 Guns."

Green Day performs during the 2009 MTV Video Music Awards.

1. R.E.M.: 12 awards

Over their 31-year career (1980–2011), this Georgia-based band released 15 albums. Considered a pioneer of alternative music, the band was equally known for its smart lyrics and lead singer Michael Stipe's unclear vocals. In 1989 they won their first MTV award for "Orange Crush." Other trophies followed for "Losing My Religion" (1991), "Man on the Moon" (1993), and "Everybody Hurts" (1994).

Did you enjoy your tour through the best of the best in music and theater?
Kind of gets you thinking about why and how an artist—or a work of art such as a
song or a Broadway show—ends up at the top, right? There are all kinds of ways
to measure success. We used sales, awards won, and theater-run length. Maybe
you have some other ideas about how to determine what and who are the best.
And who knows what the future holds for stage and sound? The next chart-topping
artist or sold-out performance could be just around the corner. Better keep your
ears open!

The Lion King ranks No. 5 in our list of longest-running Broadway shows. What other ways can you rank this musical?

Now that you've checked out our top 10 lists, it's time to make your own! First, think about your favorite songs, shows, or performers. What impresses you the most about them? How can you measure their success?

Come up with ideas for lists that spark your interest. Find out which songs in your favorite music genre spent the longest time at the top of the charts. Or see if you can track down Broadway's highest-paid stars.

Once you've got your idea for a list, it's time to do the research and find your Top Tens. Then add a few sentences about the facts you used to make your list. You might also want to add some interesting facts about the people—or places, things, or events—on your list.

Other Top Ten List Ideas

• Broadway Shows with Most Performances

• Most Viewed Music Videos

• Musical Artists with the Most Songs on the *Billboard* Hot 100 List

• Musicals with the Most Sold-Out Performances Worldwide

• Best-Selling Broadway Musical Albums

• Youngest Tony Award Winners

• Top Ten Highest-Paid Musicians

debut: the first time someone does something in public or for the public

gross: overall total income, not counting costs

meta: talking about itself

musical: a play (or movie) that tells a story with songs and often dancing

platinum: one million songs or albums sold. Double platinum means "two million sales."

producer: a person in charge of making—and usually providing the money for—a play, movie, or record

R&B: rhythm and blues, a type of music that combines elements of soul, funk, pop, and hip-hop music

revival: a new production of a play or other theater show that has not been performed recently

revolution: an attempt by many people to end or change the rule of a government

revue: a theater production made up of loosely connected funny songs, dances, and short plays

run: the period of time that a play or other theater show is performed

score: the music (but not the lyrics) for a theatrical production

Donovan, Sandy. *Movies and TV Top Tens.* Minneapolis: Lerner Publications, 2015.
Check out more top 10 lists about your favorite TV shows and movies in this fun book.

Frankos, Laura. *The Broadway Musical Quiz Book.* New York: Applause Theatre & Cinema Books, 2010.
Packed with more than a thousand trivia questions, this quiz book will keep theater fans of all ages guessing.

Grammy.com
http://www.grammy.com
Visit this fun site for photos, videos, news, and more about your favorite Grammy performances, winners, and losers.

Internet Broadway Database
http://www.ibdb.com
Check out this vast collection of information on the people, shows, theaters, songs, and everything else you want to know about Broadway.

MTV.com
http://www.mtv.com
All the buzzworthy music video news you crave—including who's most popular, most talked about, or most up-and-coming.

Tony Awards
http://www.tonyawards.com/index.html
Watch videos of past Tony Awards ceremonies, search winners and nominees, and test yourself with trivia questions about Broadway on this fun site.

PHOTO ACKNOWLEDGMENTS

The images in this book are used with the permission of:
© stevanovicigor/iStock/Thinkstock (red curtains); © Matt Kent/
Wire Image/Getty Images, pp. 4–5; Craig Robertson/ZUMA Press/
Newscom, p. 6; Tom Donoghue/Polaris/Newscom, p. 7; Alberto E.
Tamargo/Sipa USA/Newscom, p. 8; © Christopher Polk/Getty
Images, p. 9; © The Hot Ticket/Courtesy Everett Collection, p. 10;
Donna Ward/ABACAUSA.COM/Newscom, p. 11; Giancarlo
Gorassini/ABACAUSA.CO/Newscom, p. 12; © Simon Fergusson/
Getty Images, p. 13; © Jim Smeal/WireImage/Getty Images, p. 14;
© Ke.Mazur/WireImage/Getty Images, p. 15; © Gabriel Olsen/
Getty Images for Radio.com, p. 16; © Paul Natkin/WireImage/
Getty Images, p. 17; © Andrew H. Walker/WireImage for Tony
Awards Productions/Getty Images, p. 18; Dreamworks/Warner
Bros/The Kobal Collection, p. 19; © Jemal Countess/Getty Images
for Tony Awards Productions, p. 20; © John Springer Collection/
CORBIS, p. 21; © KMazur/WireImage/Getty Images, p. 22;
© Didier Messens/Getty Images, p. 23; © Jeff Kravitz/
FilmMagic/Getty Images, p. 24; © Jay West/WireImage/Getty
Images, p. 25; Roslan Rahmani/AFP/Getty Images/Newscom,
pp. 26–27.

Front cover: © Ryan McVay/The Image Bank/Getty Images
(spotlight); © stevanovicigor/iStock/Thinkstock (red curtains).

Main body text set in News Gothic MT Std Condensed 12/14.
Typeface provided by Monotype Typography.